HISTORY
AS EVIDENCE

THE
ROMANS

HISTORY AS EVIDENCE

THE
ROMANS

MIKE CORBISHLEY

Illustrated by David Salariya and Shirley Willis

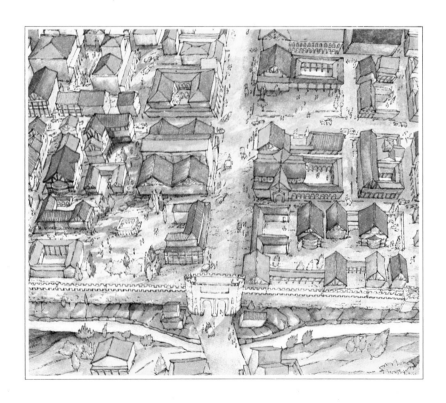

Kingfisher Books

Contents

Editor: Caroline Royds
Designer: Ben White

The publishers wish to thank the following for supplying photographs for this book: 9 Mansell Collection; 12 Italian Ministry of Defence; 15 Picturepoint; 18 Werner Forman Archive/Orti; 21 *top* Ronald Sheridan; 23 *top left* J. E. Hancock, *bottom right* Colchester and Essex Museum; 24 *top* Colchester and Essex Museum, *bottom* University of Cambridge; 26 *bottom left* M. Corbishley; 29 *top* Colchester Archaeological Trust; 31 R. Agache, Service des Fouilles.

Kingfisher Books, Grisewood & Dempsey Ltd, Elsley House, 24–30 Great Titchfield Street, London W1P 7AD

First published in paperback in 1992 by Kingfisher Books.
10 9 8 7 6 5 4 3 2 1
Originally published in hardback in 1983 by Kingfisher Books.

Copyright © Grisewood & Dempsey Ltd 1983

BRITISH LIBRARY CATALOGUING-IN-PUBLICATION DATA.
A catalogue record for this book is available from the British Library.

ISBN 0 86272 873 8

Cover design by Terry Woodley
Cover illustration by Eva Melhuish of Garden Studio
Printed and bound in Italy

Below: The country we now call Italy is very mountainous. Settlements and, later, towns grew up in the valleys with their good farming land. In the 6th century BC, the country was populated by a number of different tribes. Some groups, especially the Etruscans, Carthaginians and Greeks, took over and controlled large areas. The Latins gradually began to control the territory around them. In 509 BC they threw out their Etruscan rulers and began to form a state based on the town of Rome.

Introduction

This book is about the Romans. They began as small groups of farmers in central Italy. Rome later became an Empire in which about 60 million people lived. At one stage, someone saying 'I am a Roman citizen' could have lived on the edge of the Atlantic Ocean or on the Black Sea; in a city in North Africa or Greece, or on a farm in Spain or Holland.

Latin was the official language of the Roman Empire and most people spoke it, though some undoubtedly went on using their own language as well. Many Latin words appear in this book and you will find that, because our own language partly comes from Latin, they are often very similar to words we use today.

Two different sorts of evidence help us to discover how the Romans lived in different parts of their great Empire. One is written evidence, the histories, journals, poems, plays, even the recipe books, that have survived. The other is archaeological evidence – all the things from the past which remain, above or below ground, from buildings, roads, farms and fields, to all those objects which people throw away or lose. All this evidence can be investigated and a picture of the past will gradually emerge.

Below: The Romans gradually won over or defeated in war all the peoples in Italy itself. They also began to control other mediterranean countries until, by the 2nd century AD, all this territory was part of the Roman Empire. The provinces, as these countries were called, became part of this Empire in various ways. Egypt, for example, was the personal property of the Emperor Augustus. Many provinces, though, became Roman after invasion by the Roman army – for example, Cyprus in 58 BC, Syria in 63 BC, parts of Germany in 17 AD and Britain in 43 AD.

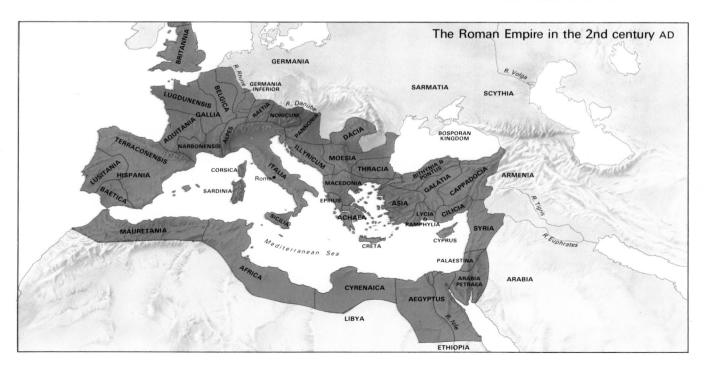

The Roman Empire in the 2nd century AD

Rome

People were living on a group of seven hills overlooking the River Tiber as early as the 8th century BC. These villages grew into the largest city in the Roman world. The magnificence of Rome's public buildings was unequalled anywhere in the Empire.

When the Romans first set up their state they called it a *res publica* – a republic. People voted in officials to carry out the job of government, often two or more for the same job to make sure that no one man was like a king and held power on his own. Women were not allowed to take part in politics at all.

Two *consuls* were elected each year to serve as 'prime ministers', chief ministers of justice and commanders of the armed forces. The *senate*, which had about 300 members and was similar to a modern parliament, advised and directed the consuls and other officials. At first there were two classes of people: the *patricians* – the privileged class, and the *plebeians* – ordinary working people. The plebeians had no say in governing the country, but they fought for equal rights, and *tribunes* were eventually elected to look after their interests in the senate.

A note about dates: Yearly dates are based today on the supposed date of the birth of Christ. The years before Christ are counted backwards – for example, Julius Caesar invaded Britain first in 55 BC, then again in 54 BC. From the birth of Christ the dates are counted forwards (AD stands for *Anno Domini* – 'in the year of the Lord'). The Romans worked out their yearly dates from the foundation of the city, or from a list of the consuls elected each year.

Below: On the back of the coin is the Emperor on horseback, with armour and weapons taken from the defeated enemy on each side. He rides on a triumphal arch built to celebrate a military victory. On the arch are the words DE BRITANNIS – 'Victory over the Britons' – reminding the Romans of Claudius' great campaign in Britain. Coins today usually have the date stamped on them. Here the date is in the letters T R P IIII on the front of the coin. Dates of official posts were always recorded at Rome and we know that this meant the year AD 44–45.

Right: Drawings of the front and back of a Roman coin. As on coins today, there was little room for writing and so words were shortened. In other words the letters on coins are a sort of code. Sort out the code and you can 'read' the coin. (The letter U is written V – it's easier to carve on inscriptions.) On the front of the coin is the head of the Emperor Claudius. Around him are his name TIBERIUS CLAUDIUS and the Emperor's official titles: CAESAR AUGUSTUS, PONTIFEX MAXIMUS ('Chief Priest of Rome') and TRIBUNICIA POTESTATE IIII ('Chief Minister for the 4th time').

A new class of people, the *equites*, emerged in the 2nd century BC – rich businessmen who did not come from the noble families of the patrician class. Citizens from all three classes could hold government office, although, because they were not paid, only the wealthy tended to become politicians. Political parties formed, and elections were usually violent occasions as supporters clashed with each other. A climax was reached in the 1st century BC with several full-scale civil wars.

Below are the portraits of three famous Roman politicians. **Gnaeus Pompeius Magnus** Pompey the Great (left). Born 106 BC, equites class, held various military and government posts, conquered new provinces for Rome in the East. Led forces against Caesar in the Civil War. Lost an important battle and was murdered on 29th September 48 BC. **Gaius Julius Caesar** (centre). Born 102 BC into the patrician class. Held important military, government and religious offices from the age of 20. Campaigned in Gaul 58–49 BC. Formed a coalition with Pompey, then campaigned against him in the Civil War. Victorious, he took more and more power for himself and became 'Dictator for Life' in 44 BC. Murdered by his political enemies on 15th March 44 BC. **Gaius Julius Caesar Octavianus Augustus** (right). Born 63 BC into the same patrician family as Caesar. After Caesar's murder, civil war broke out again, from which Augustus emerged, 14 years later, as Rome's first Emperor, calling himself 'The first citizen of Rome'. He died on 19th August AD 14 and the senate declared him a god a month later. With Augustus the period of Empire began. Elections were still held for some posts but democracy, as it had been under the republic, was not established again during the remaining 400 years of Roman rule.

Above: Roman masons were skilled craftsmen who carved stone for a variety of uses – in public buildings, statues and gravestones. Popular types of gravestones could be seen in masons' yards throughout the Empire; details were added when one was ordered for a funeral.

The City Centre

In the centre of all Roman towns were buildings for government, ceremony, religion and entertainment (1. Colosseum amphitheatre). These buildings were grouped around the *forum* – an open area where people would meet to make business deals, set up stalls to sell their goods or just chat – like a town square today. This reconstruction is of one forum in Rome called the 'Roman Forum', in the early 4th century AD. You can see statues of famous Romans and their gods in this open area. Triumphal arches were usually built to celebrate victories or to honour emperors, like the arch of Septimius Severus (2), who was Emperor in the 3rd century AD. He was born in the province of Africa and died in Eburacum (York) in Britain. The arch at (3) was built by the senate to mark the capture of Jerusalem in AD 70 by the Emperor Titus. The impressive platform (4) called the *rostra* was where politicians addressed meetings. The *curia* (5) was the meeting place for the senate. The *basilica* was a very large hall with aisles on each side, used as an indoor meeting place – for law courts, social gatherings and for business. (6) is the Basilica Aemilia and (7) the Basilica of Maxentius.

The Romans believed that gods controlled everything that happened and needed to have offerings, sacrifices (of animals) and prayers made to them. Just as a man would make offerings on behalf of his family, so the Emperor would act as priest on behalf of the country. The Romans invented some of the gods and goddesses, all of whom had special duties; others came from peoples they conquered. (8) the Temple of Vesta, the goddess of the hearth and therefore of the home, with its ever-burning fire. (9) the Temple of Romulus, mythical founder of Rome. (10) the Temple of Venus and Roma – Venus a goddess of love combined with Roma (Rome herself). (11) the Temple of Castor and Pollux twin sons of the chief Greek god Zeus. The Temple of Julius Caesar is at (12) and that of the Emperor Antoninus and his wife Faustina is at (13) – they were all made into gods. A 'sacred way' (14) runs through the forum.

Entertainment

"I happened to call in at a midday show in the amphitheatre, expecting some sport, fun and relaxation. It was just the opposite. By comparison the fights that had already taken place were merciful. Now they really get down to business – it's sheer murder. In the morning men are thrown to the lions or bears; at noon they are thrown to the spectators."

This is Seneca writing about the games in the amphitheatre in the 1st century AD. In the lunch-hour, between other contests, criminals were forced to fight each other to the death. The last man alive was kept until the same time the next day. The spectacles in the amphitheatre, which was sometimes flooded for sea-battles, were usually paid for by rich politicians or Emperors. Admission was free to everyone, even slaves.

The trained fighters-to-the-death, called *gladiators*, were usually slaves captured in war. It was possible to be set free if you fought well. There were various types of gladiators, depending on the equipment they used. Three types wore body armour: the Thracian carried a round shield and a curved dagger, the Gaul had a sword and a shield, and the Samnite, whose body was completely covered in armour, carried a rectangular shield and an axe. These heavily-armed gladiators were set against a *retiarius* who carried a net, a three-pronged spear and a dagger. He wore a shoulder-guard.

Right: The chariot races in the Circus Maximus (Great Circus) in Rome were much more like sport than the games in the Colosseum – even if the competitors were often killed. The track, 600 metres long, was straight with rounded ends. It could hold 250,000 spectators. Twelve chariots raced seven laps around the *spina* or backbone of the track. Charioteers belonged to one of four teams – Reds, Whites, Blues and Greens – which people betted madly on. The charioteer Diocles became a millionaire, winning 1462 out of 4257 races in his career. As happens today, not everyone enjoyed sport (preferring a play in the theatre perhaps). The writer Pliny said, *"The Circus Games do not interest me at all. If you've seen one race, you've seen them all"*.

Left: The Colosseum (actually called the Amphitheatrum Flavium) got its name later from a colossal statue of the Emperor Nero which stood nearby. The Roman historian Cassius Dio tells us that when the Emperor Titus completed the amphitheatre in AD 80, 9000 animals were killed during the 100 days of games. Built to hold 50,000 spectators it had 80 entrances. The floor (now gone) was of wood with a number of trap-doors which led to cages for wild animals. Men called *bestiarii* were set against these animals.

With rival entertainment offered by gladiators and charioteers it was difficult to fill the theatres in Rome, which were built for large audiences. The theatre which Pompey had built could hold 40,000 people. Nevertheless a great many people enjoyed plays and other performances in theatres all over the Roman Empire.

Both the plays and the theatres themselves were first copied from the Greeks. A theatre was built in a D-shape like half an amphitheatre (look for the theatre in the Colchester reconstruction on page 27). The audience, who got in free, would have brought cushions for the hard stone seats and were protected from the sun by awnings overhead. Some theatres even had a sprinkler system which cooled the audience with perfumed water!

Theatregoers often spent all day watching different sorts of performances – serious plays, comedies, slapstick farces or mimes. There might also be a *pantomimus* – a sort of ballet with music – or recitals of music or poems which were usually held in a small covered theatre called an *odeon*. Some Roman theatres survive (probably the best is at Orange in the south of France) and you can still read, or even see, Roman plays today.

Pompeii

After Rome itself, Pompeii is probably the best-known of Roman cities. This is because the entire town was covered, and preserved, by the eruption of the volcano Vesuvius in AD 79. After two centuries of excavation, archaeologists have still not uncovered all the town.

Even as recently as 1980 the towns and villages on the Bay of Naples were severely damaged by an earthquake. Roman writers tell us that in AD 62 Pompeii and nearby Herculaneum suffered a similar earthquake. However, that caused only minor damage compared to what happened 17 years later.

An eye-witness account of the volcanic eruption of AD 79 has survived. At the time, the Roman writer Pliny was staying with his uncle, the commander of the Roman fleet stationed at the nearby port of Misenum.

> "On 24th August, at about 1pm, my mother pointed out to my uncle an odd-shaped cloud. We couldn't make out which mountain it came from but later found out it was from Vesuvius. The cloud was rising in a shape rather like a pine tree because it shot up to a great height in the form of a tall trunk, then spread out at the top into branches."

Pliny's uncle decided at first to investigate this extraordinary cloud which he said was 'sometimes bright, sometimes dark as if full of earth and cinders'. But then he received reports that people were in danger and decided to send in the fleet to help the survivors. Pliny tells us that his uncle died, suffocated by sulphur fumes, while trying to get back to his ship.

By the time the sky had cleared three days later all the towns on the Bay of Naples had suffered. Some, like Pompeii and Herculaneum, could not be lived in again.

Above: Many fires broke out in the town when the eruption happened. Some objects not normally found on excavations – for example, bread, seeds and nuts – have been preserved because they were burnt and turned into carbon.

Right: Although objects from the towns of Pompeii and Herculaneum had turned up from time to time before, excavations did not begin until the 18th century. This illustration is from a guide book to Pompeii of 1881. It shows the uncovering of a bakery with the millstones for grinding the flour on the right and the oven in the background, complete with bread, which was ready for customers in the afternoon of 24th August AD 79.

Above: Part of the ruins of Pompeii as they are today.
Below: Both people and animals were suffocated by the volcanic fumes. Their bodies slowly rotted away inside the ash which fell and solidified into moulds around them. You can pour liquid plaster into the spaces which were left and recover almost perfect casts. This guard dog was chained up outside a house, perhaps forgotten by his owners or perhaps they too were suffocated. Favourite names for dogs were *Ferox* (Fierce) or *Celer* (Swift).

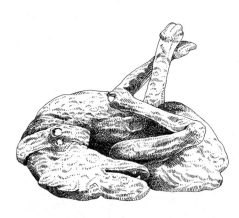

We imagine volcanoes pouring out molten lava, but Vesuvius rained ash, pumice-stone and lava-stone pebbles down onto the nearby towns. As far away as Naples, everything was covered with a thin layer of ash but Pompeii, only 8·5 km away from the volcano, was buried under nearly 4 metres of ash and stones. Herculaneum was filled with a mudflow caused by the eruption.

From a population of 20,000, about 2000 people died at Pompeii. The town itself could not be lived in again and, after the Roman period, was forgotten. It was rediscovered in the 18th century and archaeological work began. A new director of excavations, Giuseppe Fiorelli, was appointed in 1860. He worked very carefully, uncovering whole streets instead of individual buildings, and also invented the technique of taking plaster casts, like the dog on the left. As the aerial view above shows, the streets of Pompeii divided the town into regular blocks called *insulae* (the word means islands). At the time of the eruption, it had two theatres, an amphitheatre, three public baths and a number of temples and administrative buildings.

There was a town at Pompeii long before the Romans took over this part of Italy, and for some time it was a prosperous Greek town. It was settled in 80 BC as a *colonia* (a sort of new-town) for retired soldiers and their families. During the 1st century AD it became a rich trading town which sold, among other things, millstones (there was plenty of local lava-stone), a sauce made from fish, perfumes and cloth. Market day was Saturday. How many different sorts of shops can you see in the street scene on the next page?

The Baths

"I live over the public baths – you know what that means. Ugh! It's sickening. First there are the 'strongmen' doing their exercises and swinging heavy lead weights about with grunts and groans. Next there are the lazy ones having a cheap massage – I can hear someone being slapped on the shoulders. Then there is the noise of a brawler or a thief being arrested and the man who always likes the sound of his own voice in the bath. And what about the ones who leap into the pool making a huge splash as they hit the water!"

Unless they actually lived over a bath-house, not many people would have agreed with Lucius Seneca who wrote this around AD 63. A bath-house was considered essential in any Roman town and most towns had more than one. Everyone went to the baths – it was cheap enough for both rich and poor to go frequently and children got in free. But it is a mistake to think that the Romans went to the baths simply to get clean. That was only one part of an enjoyable way to spend several hours. The baths were somewhere to meet friends for a chat, a game of dice or to sort out some business deal.

As the plan on the right shows, baths were very complicated. They were not all identical but each one had to have an *apodyterium*, to undress and leave your clothes in, and a *tepidarium* – a warm room to gradually get you used to the *caldarium* – the hot room. This would not only be hot but also steamy like a modern Turkish bath. The floors of these rooms would be heated by a *hypocaust* – an underfloor heating system. In the caldarium there would be baths of hot water sunk into the floor and there might even be a *laconicum* – a very hot dry room like a sauna. From the hot rooms you would go into the *frigidarium* – the cold room – and plunge into a small pool of cold water or even swim in a larger pool. There was also a courtyard for exercise, or just for strolling in, called a *palaestra*.

Right: A plan of one of the three public baths at Pompeii. This one, the smallest, is next to the forum. Men and women did not bathe together and bath-houses usually had separate sessions for each. You will see that these baths have a separate entrance and bath rooms for women. A large staff of slaves would be needed for all sorts of jobs – keeping the baths clean and the fires going, serving snacks and drinks, massaging or even plucking hair from the armpits of customers. An essential job was to scrape the customers clean after a hot steamy bath or exercise. They rubbed oil over the skin and scraped off the dirt with a curved metal instrument called a *strigilis*. In the palaestra you might find some of the people Seneca complained about, doing their strenuous exercises. Some might also be playing *trigon* – a game in which three players stood in a triangle throwing balls quickly to one another.

Right: The *caldarium* or hot room of the baths near the forum. The people of Pompeii loved scribbling on walls, and the baths were a favourite place for these scribbles, called *graffiti*. Someone who had been gambling in a nearby town has written: "I had a good win at Nuceria, playing dice – and I didn't cheat!". Some of the graffiti was useful information, for example the market days in local towns; some was rather more personal: "Successus the cloth-weaver loves Iris, the innkeeper's slave-girl."

1. Men's entrance
2. Women's entrance
3. Slaves' entrance
4. Apodyterium
5. Frigidarium
6. Tepidarium
7. Caldarium
8. Palaestra
9. Furnaces

Houses and Flats

In Pompeii, as in other Roman towns, the house you lived in depended on how wealthy you were. If you were rich your house would have a large number of rooms, perhaps twenty or thirty, for your family and your house-slaves. Because the Romans liked to be as private as possible inside their houses, they often had no windows on the outside walls, at least downstairs. This also made burglary difficult. The 'living' rooms and bedrooms would be well furnished and decorated with painted walls – the Roman equivalent of wallpaper, and with mosaics covering the floors. Mosaics were patterns or pictures made up of hundreds of tiny cubes of stone and brick set in mortar.

Roman houses had no front gardens and the front door or gate was on the street. You might well be greeted with a mosaic floor showing a fierce-looking dog and the words *cave canem* – Beware of the Dog! The dog, if there was one, would be looked after by the doorman who kept unwelcome or uninvited visitors away. Once past the dog and the doorman you would be standing in the *atrium*, a large room with an enormous open skylight. This not only let in much needed light but also the rain, and so immediately below was an ornamental pool – an *impluvium*. Around the atrium were bedrooms, storerooms and slaves' quarters. At the end of the front part of the house would be the *tablinum*, open to the atrium and the back part of the house by means of hinged or sliding wooden doors. This was the main room of the house, rather like our 'living' room.

Below: The garden, with its small trees, shrubs, and herbs for the kitchen, at the back of the house of the Vettii, a family of rich merchants. An open corridor with columns provided a cool pleasant walkway and protected the rooms around from bad weather. Here you would find bedrooms and a *triclinium* – the dining room where low couches were set out for the diners to recline at meals. This house had several dining rooms, placed to catch the light at different times of the year. Part of the house at least would probably have had an upper storey, and there would also have been a kitchen, and a small room where the family's gods were kept. Some of the rooms were heated by the house's *hypocaust* system.

"There's no peace and quiet in the city for a poor man. Early in the morning schoolmasters stop us from having any normal life. Before it gets light we have the bakers, then it's the hammering of the copper-smiths all day."

The poet Martial wrote this while living in his third floor flat in Rome. Blocks of flats for those who could not afford houses were built in most Roman cities. In Rome they were five or six storeys high. At Pompeii, where there was more room, flats were usually only two or three storeys high. They were often badly constructed (sometimes they just fell down), and were mainly built of wood, so the risk of fire was great.

Shopkeepers and craftsmen probably lived in these flats (right) in Ostia, a port 26 kilometres from Rome. They would also have lived above the shops lining the street in the market day scene reconstructed on pages 16–17. As well as workshops for craftsmen and one-room schools, there would have been take-away hot food shops, because many of the residents of flats could not cook at home. The Romans liked their food with lots of spices and herbs. Here is a recipe for sauce for boiled ostrich from Marcus Apicius' recipe book written in the 1st century AD:

"Bring to the boil in a saucepan pepper, mint, roasted cumin, parsley-seed, dates, honey, vinegar, cooking wine, fish stock and a little oil. Thicken the sauce with cornflour and pour over the pieces of ostrich in a serving dish and sprinkle with pepper."

Above: Blocks of flats at Ostia. Below: No poor family could afford this sort of kitchen. The cook, a slave, is standing by the stove, and all around there are pots and pans – some pottery, some of bronze and iron. There are very large pots for keeping wine, oil, olives and fish sauce in. Every kitchen had a *mortarium* for grinding up all the spices used in Roman cooking.

Fort to Town

When an Emperor decided to conquer a new province or to campaign against an enemy, he had a large professional army to call upon. But the military rule was replaced by a civilian administration as soon as possible, and the conquered people were encouraged to build towns like those in other parts of the Empire.

"The light-armed auxiliary troops and archers led the march to repel sudden enemy attacks. Next marched a troop of heavy-armed Roman soldiers, infantry and cavalry. They were followed by ten men from each centuria carrying their own kit and the equipment for marking out the camp. After them came the roadmakers to straighten the road."

This account of the Roman army invading Galilee in AD 67 was part of a work by the Jewish historian Josephus. Behind the commander came the crack troops, the cavalry, then the catapults and battering rams for sieges. Next came the officers, the standards (sacred emblems and flags of each unit) and then the trumpeters. Behind them came the main army and equipment.

The army was divided into a number of *legions* with about 5500 legionaries in each, including about 120 cavalry. A *centurion* commanded each *centuria* – literally 100 men. Legionaries had to be Roman citizens to enlist. A large number of auxiliary troops were recruited from the provinces. They became Roman citizens after 25 years of service.

Below: In AD 114 the Emperor Trajan built a carved column to celebrate his victory over the Dacians. These fragments of the column show (left) the army moving from the camp's gateway onto a pontoon bridge, carrying the standards of each centuria; and (right) the troops attacking an enemy camp. The legionaries are protected by locking their shields together. They called this a *testudo* – the word means a tortoiseshell.

Left: This aerial view shows the remains of a town defended by earth banks and ditches, built by people who lived in Britain before the Romans invaded. Such towns are often called hill-forts. This site is Hod Hill in Dorset. There were perhaps 270 circular houses in this small, well-planned town, with a population of nearly 1000. After its capture in AD 44, the Roman army engineers built a temporary fort, using part of the existing defences, which covered about 4 hectares in the north-west corner of the town.

The main role of the army was to protect the Roman Empire, but it was also used to capture new areas. Julius Caesar, as governor of the province in northern Italy, began in 58 BC to conquer Gallia. During these campaigns he invaded Britain twice, in 55 and 54 BC. Although both invasions were short and he was unable to win a new province, he did collect useful information about Britain and the people there. He wrote,

> "All the Britons paint themselves with a blue dye called woad; this gives them a more frightening appearance in battle. They wear their hair long and the men have moustaches. The population is very large and there are very many farmhouses similar to those the Gauls build. There is a large number of cattle. Tin is found inland and small quantities of iron near the coast. There is timber of every kind."

It was not until the reign of the Emperor Claudius that Caesar's information could be put to good use. In the autumn of AD 43, Claudius' invasion commander, Aulus Plautius, led a force of four legions (about 40,000 soldiers in all) across the Channel. The army fought its way to the River Thames and waited over a month for Claudius himself to arrive. Claudius led the army, together with some elephants to impress the 'natives', to Colchester, then the capital of south-eastern Britain.

Claudius had no trouble taking the town even though the area enclosed by its defences covered 19 square kilometres. He left almost immediately for Rome, after only 16 days in Britain, and the army set about building its camps. They were temporary ones at first; then, after part of the invasion force had been sent off to conquer the south and west, a more permanent fort was built for the Twentieth Legion. The cavalry officer Longinus (right), from Bulgaria, died in AD 48 at Colchester. His gravestone shows him on horseback over a cowering and naked Briton. Everyone who saw this in the cemetery knew that the might of Rome had arrived.

Above: The inscription on this gravestone, from one of Colchester's Roman cemeteries, can be translated as: "Longinus Sdapeze, son of Matygus, a junior officer from the First Thracian Cavalry Squadron, from the district of Sardica, aged 40, served 15 years, lies buried here. His heirs set this up as directed in his will."

Forts and Frontiers

Above: an X-ray photograph of a dagger like those carried by the legionaries, found at Colchester. It is made of iron with a wooden handle. The X-ray has revealed the silver inlay on the scabbard.

"The infantry have armour to protect the chest and a helmet, and carry a blade on each side – a sword and a dagger. The infantry picked to form the general's bodyguard carry a spear and a round shield but the other soldiers carry an oblong shield. Soldiers also carry a saw, basket, pick, axe, strap, bill-hook, chain and three days' rations."

No wonder Josephus goes on to say that the Roman foot-soldier was 'almost as heavily weighed-down as a pack mule'. In all, he might carry as much as 30 kilograms on the march. He wore a woollen tunic under his armour, sandals with hob-nailed soles and a thick woollen cloak. With all this equipment and armour, he was ready to fight on the march and build a camp at the end of the day. We know that an army could be expected to cover 30 kilometres in about five hours (with some breaks).

The rest of the invasion force – those not garrisoned in Colchester or keeping the route from the south coast secure in case of retreat – marched off to gain control of as much of Britain as they could. The first 'push' was to the south-west where, by AD 47, the Romans had secured a frontier from the River Humber in the north to Gloucester on the River Severn and through to Exeter. They pushed into Wales and northern Britain and by the late 70s had established permanent forts there and begun to build towns for the civilian population. This was closely followed by a further 'push' against the tribes in Scotland. The army engineers planned out fast routes through the countryside, and soldiers helped to build the roads.

But tackling the warlike tribes in Scotland proved difficult for the Roman army. The Emperor Hadrian, who visited Britain in AD 122, decided on a drastic course of action to keep out the 'barbarians', as the Romans called them. He began the construction of a great stone wall, stretching 120 kilometres, from the Tyne to the Solway Firth. Anyone wanting to get across Hadrian's Wall into the province of Britain had to cross a deep ditch, climb a wall 6 metres high, cross a well-patrolled road then tackle the *vallum* – a large ditch with an earth bank on each side.

The reconstruction below is of Chesters Fort, one of the seventeen permanent forts built on or close to the Wall. It covers about 2.3 hectares and was built for a cavalry regiment of 500 men. Inside the strong wall, with its gates and towers, the area is divided by wide streets. Josephus says that a camp 'seems like a town suddenly sprung up'. On the northern side, facing out from the Wall, were barracks and stables. The soldiers had to be ready to ride out to attack the enemy. In the central part of the fort was the headquarters building, containing offices, a shrine which housed altars and statues of the regiment's gods, the standards, and a strong room for the soldiers' pay. Close by was the house of the commandant with its own private bath-house. Elsewhere were more barracks, food-stores, cook-houses, a hospital, workshops and lavatories. Outside the fort was a small civilian village.

Below: The Roman name for Chesters Fort was Cilurnum which means something like 'the deep pool in a river'. The River North Tyne runs nearby. The barracks, headquarters, commandant's house, wall and gates of the fort can all be seen today. Outside the fort is the bath-house for the whole regiment (one compensation for the bad weather!), Hadrian's Wall and the stone supports for a bridge. The site is open most of the year and has a museum.

Below left: An aerial view of the Roman route now called Dere Street at Chew Green in Northumberland. There are traces of the temporary and practice camps built by different units as they passed through into Scotland.

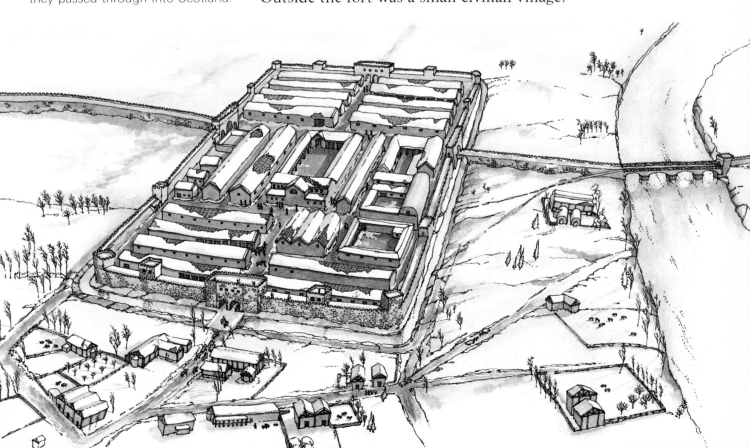

A Town in the Provinces

COLCHESTER IN THE 2ND CENTURY AD
Unlike Pompeii, Roman Colchester lies underneath the modern town. Archaeological evidence must be excavated (usually before re-building or new roads) although some Roman structures are still standing. We still do not know where the forum, basilica, baths and amphitheatre were. Colchester certainly had them and the reconstruction shows their most likely positions. 1. The road from London leads up to the town's main gate. Other gates are shown at 2, 3, 4, 5 and 6. The gates and the stone and tile wall were built around AD 125. Some of the wall still stands nearly 3m high in places. 7. The crossing of the town's main shopping streets. 8. The huge temple for worshipping the Emperor Claudius. It stands in its own precinct or courtyard. 9. Theatre. 10. Forum and basilica (?) 11. Bath-house (?) 12. Amphitheatre (?) 13. A small temple to worship both Roman and British gods.
The aerial photograph below shows Colchester today. Look closely and you will see that the shape of the Roman town is still there – even the main street then is the High Street today. The Roman walls mean that the modern road system has to go around the town.

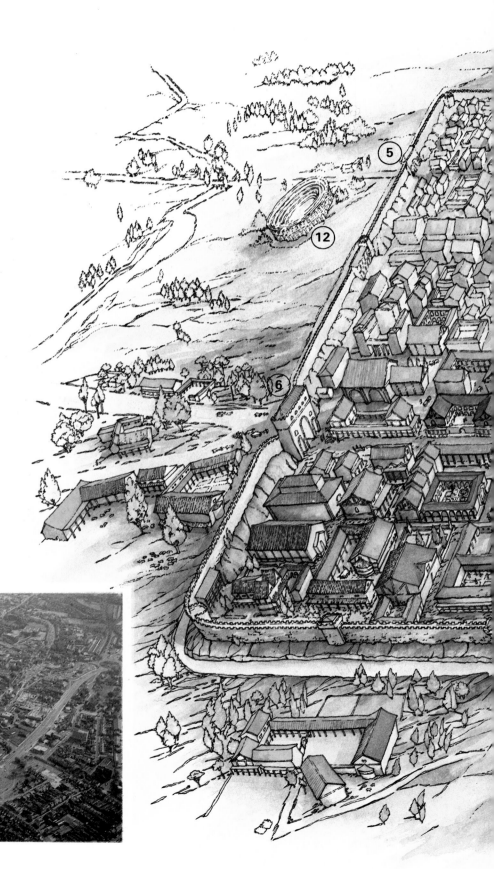

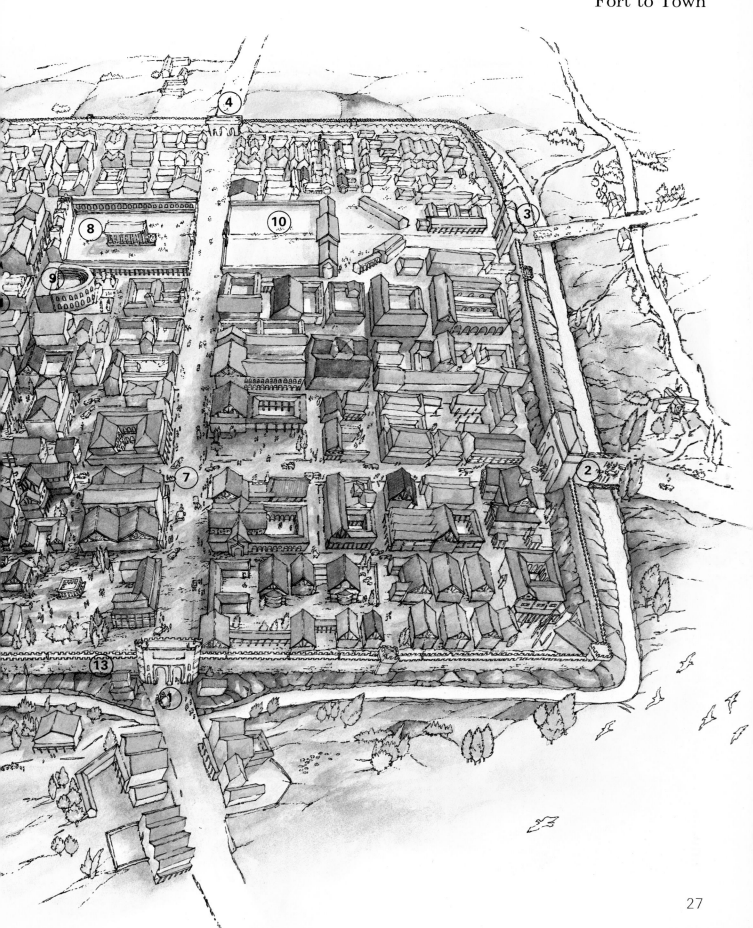

Buildings and Cemeteries

The Romans were forced to control the northern frontier of Britain by maintaining permanent garrisons, but this was not the way they wanted to run a province. As soon as an area was settled, the tribe there was encouraged to build towns and to become 'Romans'. The town council, called the *ordo*, a local version of the senate, would press the governor of the province to provide a good road system so that they could travel and trade in safety.

For the town itself the council wanted a defensive wall and gates. Inside, it had to be carefully laid out to provide the insulae or regular blocks for houses, shops and small factories. Public buildings were needed – temples, a forum, town hall, magistrates' court, market places, a theatre and perhaps even an amphitheatre. Aqueducts were built to carry water for houses and industry, for the bath-houses and lavatories. An efficient system of sewers was also very important for the health of the town. Money for all this came from taxes and government grants.

Some towns, like Colchester, grew up on the sites of forts which had been dismantled when the army pulled out of them; others were deliberately developed on the sites of former tribal settlements. By AD 49 the area around Colchester seemed peaceful, and the Twentieth Legion was posted to Gloucester. It was decided that a *colonia* – a new town for retired soldiers – was to be built where their fort had been.

Below: When a person died the body was carried on a bier in a procession to the cemetery which had, by law, to be outside the town's walls. Trumpeters or flute players led paid mourners and dancers; relatives walked behind. In Roman Britain, bodies were cremated at first but from the middle of the 2nd century AD it became the custom to bury the dead. Food and drink was sometimes placed with the remains for their final journey to the underworld. Roman gravestones often had the words DIS MANIBUS carved on them, meaning 'To the Gods of the Dead'. There is usually little room for much writing and so the words are put closely together or shortened. For example, H.S.E on Longinus' gravestone (p 23) means he, or in another case it could be she, lies buried here. You will find Roman gravestones in many museums today.

There was a ready-made population, perhaps as many as 1000 people, for the new town. As legionaries retired from the Twentieth Legion they were given land to farm (about 12.6 hectares each) around Colchester. Some of them would have settled in the village which grew up outside the fort when it was in use – perhaps to be near old comrades. These retired soldiers were Roman citizens and they expected to be able to settle down in a civilized part of the world. As inhabitants of the new town, they set a good example of how a Roman ought to live. Some married locals and gradually society changed. Sons and daughters whose fathers had been Roman soldiers from Bulgaria, Spain or Germany, and whose mothers had known earlier rulers in Colchester, were now brought up to be Roman.

Below: This Roman couple (man on the right, woman on the left), who died in the early 4th century AD, were buried in one of Colchester's cemeteries. Their bodies, in wooden coffins, were placed in a wooden vault which may have had an elaborate *mausoleum* or tomb built above. They are middle-aged and about average height. Recent excavations in Cirencester showed that the average height in Roman times was 158 cm for women and 168 cm for men.

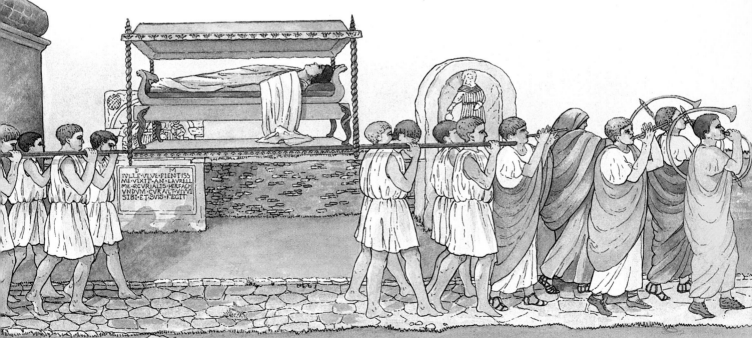

In the Countryside

The Romans used as much of the countryside as they could for growing the food needed to support all the people who lived in the towns. However, the country was also the place where the rich built splendid houses to holiday in.

The Romans used the word *villa* to mean a number of things – a house in the country, a farmhouse, a farm or a farming estate. Many wealthy Romans living in towns all over the Empire owned farms but they often had a house, or houses, in the country which they could use for holidays.

The writer Pliny owned several estates in various parts of Italy. On a tour of these estates he recommended the peace of the countryside in a letter to a friend saying 'Why not take the first opportunity to leave the noise, the senseless hullabaloo and useless effort of Rome and do some writing or just take a holiday?'. Besides his farming estates, Pliny also owned country houses with no farms attached. He describes one, which was only 29 kilometres from Rome and right on the coast, in a letter to his friend Gallus:

> "The house is the right size for me and not expensive to keep up. First you go into the atrium . . . from there into D-shaped colonnades enclosing a small but pleasant courtyard . . . there is a rather nice dining room which juts out onto the shore. All around the dining room are folding doors or big windows . . . from the back you can see the woods and in the distance the hills."

The villa at Warfusée-Abancourt has not been excavated but it is clear from the aerial photograph opposite and from the field itself, which has produced a mass of building materials, that we

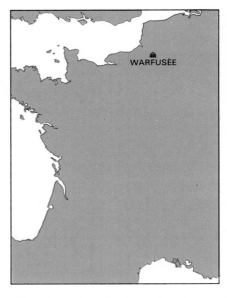

Why do archaeologists take photographs from the air? Often an aerial photograph shows how the crop has been affected by what its roots are growing in. Ditches and holes which have filled up will help the crop grow stronger or taller. It is easy to see why the crop growing over foundations is not as tall as the rest of the field. 'Crop-marks' often show in fields of wheat, barley and sugar-beet, but can sometimes be seen in grass as well. The sun's rays, at a low angle in the early morning or late afternoon, highlight these differences in the crop and make them easy to see from an aeroplane.

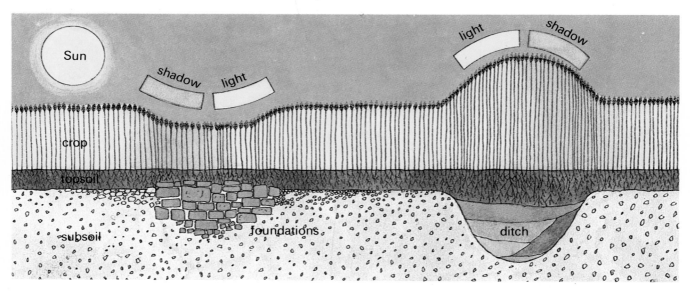

are looking at a whole range of rooms and buildings for different purposes. What we cannot see in the photograph are the fields, for animals and crops, which lie all around the villa itself.

Pliny's country house had over forty rooms as well as gardens and terraces. There were a number of bedrooms, living rooms and a library. The large kitchen was near the storerooms and the quarters for the house-slaves. Some of these slaves would have lived in all the year round to look after the house. There was a bath block with all the usual hot and cold rooms.

To build such a splendid house Pliny needed his farms to make a good profit. Most of the villas which have been investigated by archaeologists were working farms, though some include fine houses for the owners. The size of the farmhouse and farm buildings depended not only on the wealth of the owner but also on what the farm itself produced. Some went in for a variety of produce – animals, crops, fruit and vegetables; others specialised in one product. Certain estates in Britain had only cattle, some in southern France only wine, others in Africa only olives and olive oil. At one time, much of the corn needed for Rome's bread supply came from Egypt.

Above: An aerial photograph of a Roman villa at Warfusée-Abancourt. It is 22 kilometres east of the town of Amiens in France. The Romans called Amiens Samarobriva in the province of Gallia. This villa is 320 metres in length and consists of a large number of rooms built around a central courtyard and gardens. An archaeologist, Roger Agache, has discovered over 1000 villas like this in northern France from the air. Some show as crop-marks; this one shows the white stone and mortar of the villa's walls brought to the surface after deep ploughing in the winter.

A Farm

Evidence from both archaeological investigation and Roman writings provide the details needed to create this reconstruction of a villa. It is based on villas like the one found at Warfusée-Abancourt.

A great deal of information about Roman farming comes from the writer Lucius Columella. He came from the town of Gades, now Cadiz, in southern Spain. He served as an officer in the army in Syria and Cilicia and settled near Rome to farm. His main work called *About Farming* was written in about AD 60. He wrote:

"A farm should be in a healthy climate, with fertile soil, with some flat ground and some hilly on an eastern or southern slope, which is not too steep. The villa should have three sections: the villa urbana – that is the house of the owner, the villa rustica – the house of the farm manager and labourers and the villa fructuaria – the storehouse. The villa urbana should have both winter and summer rooms. The baths should face the setting of the sun in the summer to keep them lighted from noon until evening. The villa rustica should

have a high kitchen . . . little rooms for the slaves. For cattle there should be stables which can be used in both hot and cold weather. Rooms for the herdsmen and shepherds should be next to the animals they look after. The villa fructuaria should have rooms for oil, for the presses, for wine . . . hay-lofts . . . granaries .

You can see the fine house of the owner, with its columns and formal garden. Where do you think the villa rustica is?
Look for a small formal garden outside its front door.

The Farm Worker

The Romans used slaves to do most of the jobs on the farm, both in the house and outbuildings and in the fields. Life was obviously hard for most of them, and some bitterly resented being slaves or doing such hard work and tried to escape. Such slaves would be worked in a chain-gang, and kept chained at night as well.

Whether the owner lived on the estate or not, he needed someone to manage the everyday running of the farm. Lucius Columella says that the farm manager, called a *vilicus*, 'must be someone who has been hardened by farm-work since childhood and tested by practical experience'. Even though the vilicus needed all the qualities which we would expect in a farm manager today, he would be a slave himself. Another writer about agriculture, Marcus Cato, says this of the vilicus:

> "The farm manager must not be an idler, he must always be sober and must not go out to dine. He must be the first to rise in the morning and last to bed. Before that he must see that the farm is shut up and that everyone is asleep in the right place and that the animals have fodder."

In charge of the household and the slaves who worked in the house was the *vilica* or housekeeper. She would also be a slave. Cato says, "See to it that the housekeeper performs all her duties. She must be clean herself and keep the farm neat and clean. She must clean and tidy the fire-place every night before she goes to bed." Cato also recommends the amounts of food to be given to the labourers: "Each slave in the chain-gang should have 1·5 kilos of bread each day during the winter and 2 kilos when they begin to work in the vineyard." He says that the labourers should be issued with rations of wine, various relishes (like windfall olives and fish-sauce), oil and salt, and adds that a tunic, cloak and a stout pair of wooden shoes should be given to each worker every other year.

Below: Roman farm tools with reconstructed handles from a display in the National Museum of Antiquities of Scotland, Edinburgh. All the tools were found during the excavation of the fort at Newstead, Roxburghshire. 1. Iron scythe for cutting corn. 2. Rake with iron prongs set into oak. 3. Turf cutter used by the army for constructing ramparts around forts. 4. Called a mower's anvil, this solid iron peg was driven into the ground. The iron spiral stops it sinking right in. The corn mower held the scythe blade on this anvil to hammer it flat before sharpening. 5. Rake made from the antler of a red deer. When repairs were needed or new tools had to be made, there may have been labourers on the farm skilled enough to do the work. If not, smiths would be hired. Bringing their own equipment, they would come to stay (perhaps in a nearby field), build furnaces, and make whatever was required.

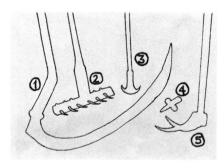

Right: Sacks of grapes being brought from the vineyard. From a mosaic floor in a house in Augusta, now Paphos, the Roman capital of the island of Cyprus.
"Get everything ready that is needed for making the wine. Wash out the vats and repair the baskets. Gather the not-so-good grapes for the coarse wine for the workers to drink." Marcus Cato.

Left: From a 1st century BC tomb in Germany. It shows a farmer taking produce to market past a roadside shrine.
"If there are towns or villages in the neighbourhood, or even rich estates, from which you can buy what you need for the farm . . . you can sell your surplus." Marcus Varro.

Right: From a 3rd century AD tomb in Rome. A farmworker is milking a goat into a clay pot.
"Cheese should be made of pure milk which is as fresh as possible. Some mix in crushed green pine-kernels and curdle it, but you can make different flavoured cheese by adding any seasoning you like." Lucius Columella.

Left: From a bronze model, only 5cm high, of a ploughman with two oxen. Found in Piercebridge, County Durham, it was perhaps made in Gaul in the 2nd or 3rd century AD.
"Some land, when you have ploughed it with oxen and plough, must be ploughed again before you plant the seed." Marcus Varro.

Archaeology in Britain

If you want to learn about archaeology, go to your local museum to find out about museum clubs for young people, or ask at the library for information about local societies. There is also a national club for young people interested in archaeology called the Young Archaeologists Club, which offers a variety of archaeological activities, a magazine and holidays. If you would like more details, send a stamped addressed envelope to Kate Pretty, New Hall, Cambridge CB3 0DF.

Young Archaeologists Club members can sometimes take part in excavations but you may be able to join a 'dig' in your own area. *Never* dig on your own or go treasure hunting. Treasure hunters do not care about the past, only the objects they dig up. Treasure hunters with metal detectors often dig into archaeological sites (even those protected by law) and so destroy the evidence for the past which you have read about in this book. They often damage our environment as well.

If you want to know more about the sorts of things an archaeologist does, send a stamped addressed envelope to the Education Officer, Council for British Archaeology, 112 Kennington Road, London SE11 6RE.

A variety of remains survive in some Roman towns which lie under modern towns – remains such as walls, gates, houses, baths, temples and other public buildings as well as hypocausts and mosaic floors. Often there will be a museum to visit as well. Good Roman **towns** to visit are London, Colchester, Lincoln, St Albans, York, Caerwent (Gwent), Exeter, Leicester, Wall (Staffordshire), Bath, Dorchester, Cirencester and Canterbury. Two towns with remains to be seen were not built over in later times – Silchester (near Reading) and Wroxeter (near Shrewsbury).

There are Roman **forts** at the Lunt (Baginton, Warwickshire), Chester, Caerleon (Gwent), Caernarfon (Gwynedd), Caer Gybi (Anglesey), Burgh Castle (Norfolk), Richborough (Kent), Pevensey (Sussex), Portchester (Hampshire), Hardknott (Cumbria), High Rochester (Northumberland). A good section of Hadrian's Wall to visit is at Walltown Crags and forts at Corbridge, Chesters, Carrawburgh (temple of the god Mithras), Housesteads, Vindolanda and Birdoswald. Further north are the remains of the earth defences of the Antonine Wall which was a defended frontier similar to Hadrian's Wall built between the Firth of Forth and the River Clyde in AD 142–3. A fort on the wall to

Roman roads were famous for being well-built and following the most direct route.

visit is Rough Castle (Stirlingshire). Other forts to visit in Scotland are Ardoch and Inchtuthil in Perthshire and Burnswark in Dumfries and Galloway.

There are remains of Roman **villas** at Lullingstone (Kent), Fishbourne (Sussex), Bignor (Sussex), Chedworth (Gloucestershire), Kings Weston (Gloucestershire), North Leigh (Oxfordshire), Rockbourne (Hampshire), Littlecote (Wiltshire), Newport and Brading on the Isle of Wight. Roman **villages** to visit are Chysauster (Cornwall) and Holyhead Hut Circles (Anglesey).

The **roads** originally built by the Romans often survive under modern roads, but some of the actual Roman surface can be seen at Blackpool Bridge (Gloucestershire), Blackstone Edge (W Yorkshire) and Wheeldale Moor (N Yorkshire). Other remains to visit are Roman **burial mounds** at Bartlow Hills (Cambridgeshire) and Mersea Island (Essex), a **bath-house** at Welwyn (Hertfordshire), a **lighthouse** and a finely preserved **house** at Dover (Kent), and a **gold-mine** at Dolaucothi (Dyfed).

Hadrian's Wall

Bibliography

Here are some reference books which you may find useful:
Imperial Rome by Alan Sorrell and Anthony Birley (Lutterworth) 1970
Pompeii by Ian Andrews (Cambridge University Press) 1978
Roman Forts by Roger Wilson (Constable) 1980
The Roman Army by John Wilkes (Cambridge University Press) 1972
The Roman Army by Peter Connolly (Macdonald) 1975
Roman Britain by John Wacher (Dent) 1978
Roman Britain – Life in an imperial province by Keith Branigan (Readers Digest) 1980
Town Life in Roman Britain by Mike Corbishley (Harraps) 1981
The Observer's Book of Ancient and Roman Britain by Harold Priestley (Warne) 1976
Roman Remains in Britain by Roger Wilson (Constable) 1980
Roman Britain by Graham Webster (Observer Maps) 1978

Above: Hadrian (AD 76—138),
Proclaimed Emperor AD 117. He built
Hadrian's Wall, as a line of defence. It
was 120 km long.

Above right: Claudius (10 BC—AD 54),
proclaimed Emperor AD 41. He
invaded Britain in AD 43.

Right: Constantine I (AD 272—337),
proclaimed Emperor AD 306. He
made Constantinople the new capital
of the Roman Empire.

A good way to find out how people lived in the Roman period is to read stories
about them. Here are some you might try about the Romans in Britain:
The Eagle of the Ninth by Rosemary Sutcliff (Oxford University Press or Penguin) 1954
The Silver Branch by Rosemary Sutcliff (Oxford University Press or Penguin) 1957
Legions of the Eagle by Henry Treece (Bodley Head or Penguin) 1954
Song for a Dark Queen by Rosemary Sutcliff (Pelham or Knight) 1978
To Spare the Conquered by Stephanie Plowman (Methuen or Penguin) 1960
The Lantern Bearers by Rosemary Sutcliff (Oxford University Press) 1979
Frontier Wolf by Rosemary Sutcliff (Oxford University Press) 1980
Spring Tide by Mary Ray (Faber & Faber) 1969

Index